For my cousins and our shared memories of Paul—P.C.

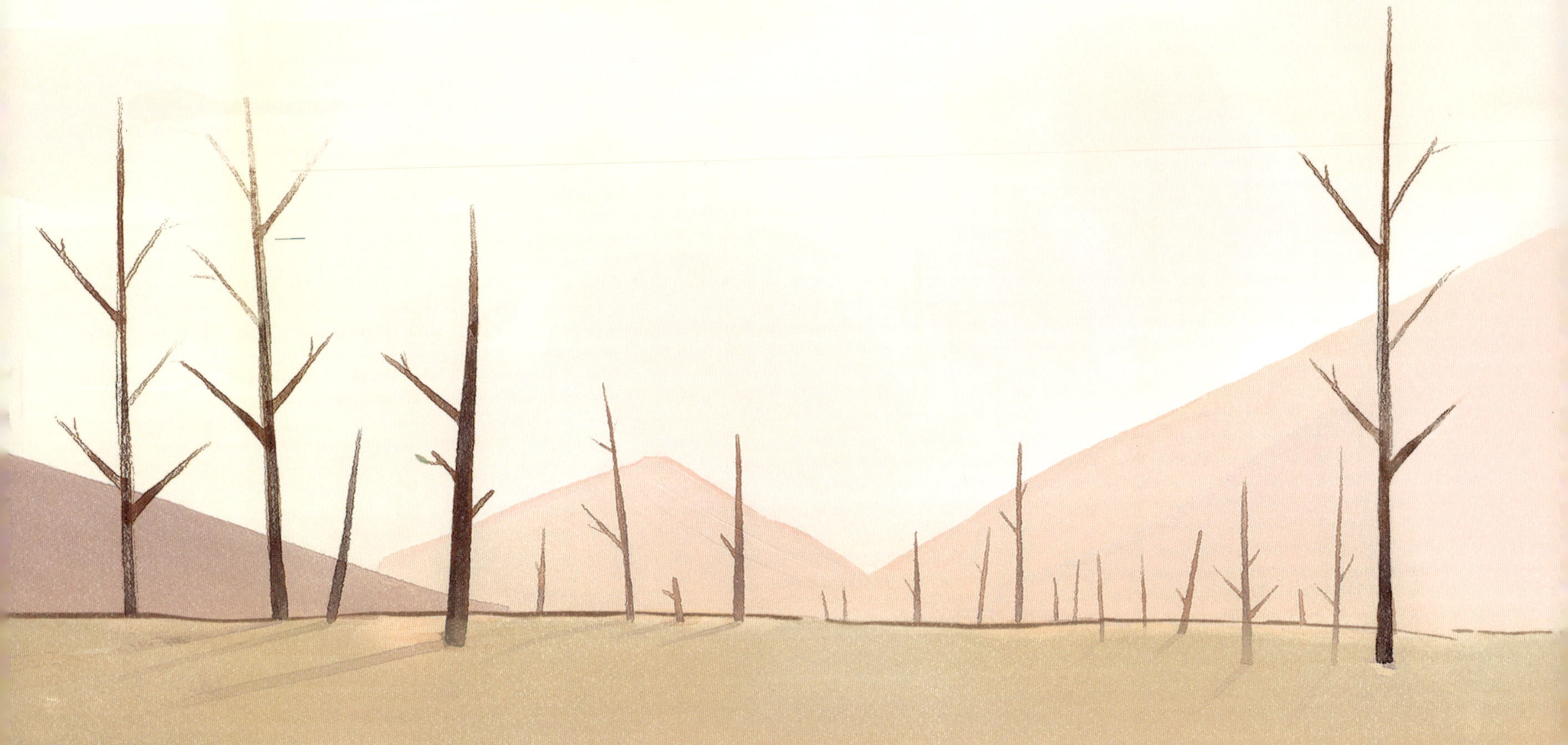

Scholastic Press
An imprint of Scholastic Australia Pty Limited (ABN 11 000 614 577)
PO Box 579 Gosford NSW 2250
www.scholastic.com.au

Part of the Scholastic Group
Sydney · Auckland · New York · Toronto · London · Mexico City
New Delhi · Hong Kong · Buenos Aires · Puerto Rico

First published by Scholastic Australia in 2017.
This edition published in 2022.

Shane DeVries created the illustrations in this book digitally.

Book design by Nicole Stofberg.

Typeset in ITC Esprit.

A catalogue record for this book is available from the National Library of Australia

ISBN: 978-1-76112-489-1

Printed in China by Ink Asia.

Scholastic Australia's policy, in association with Ink Asia, is to use papers that are renewable and made efficiently from wood grown in responsibly managed forests, so as to minimise its environmental footprint.

10 9 8 7 6 5 23 24 25 26 / 2

PHIL CUMMINGS SHANE DEVRIES

A Scholastic Press book from Scholastic Australia

Once there was a king who lived high on a hill. His castle looked over the valley to the mountains beyond.

He was a powerful man with many brave knights.

CLiNG
CLiNG
CLONG
CLONG
CLiNG
CLONG!
CLiNG
CLONG
CLANG!
tiNG!

The mountains were once rich with trees, but a powerful dragon had destroyed much of the forest with his fiery breath.

In a small village on the edge of the burnt forest lived Boy.

Boy couldn't hear, but he was happy. He spoke with dancing hands and he drew pictures for people in the sand.

His parents loved his stories . . .

but the villagers didn't understand.

'What a strange child,' they would say as they walked on by.

ROAR!
CHA
CLiNG CLONG
CLANG!

Since the forest had been burnt,
the king and the dragon had fought many fierce battles.
There was roaring,
flapping,
running about,
hiding,
dodging,
weaving
and a lot of shouting.

Boy couldn't hear the battle cries, but he had seen the fear in his mother's eyes and felt it in his father's hands when he held him close.

The battles were loud and long . . .

but no-one ever won.

One day, when the king and the dragon were battling once more . . .

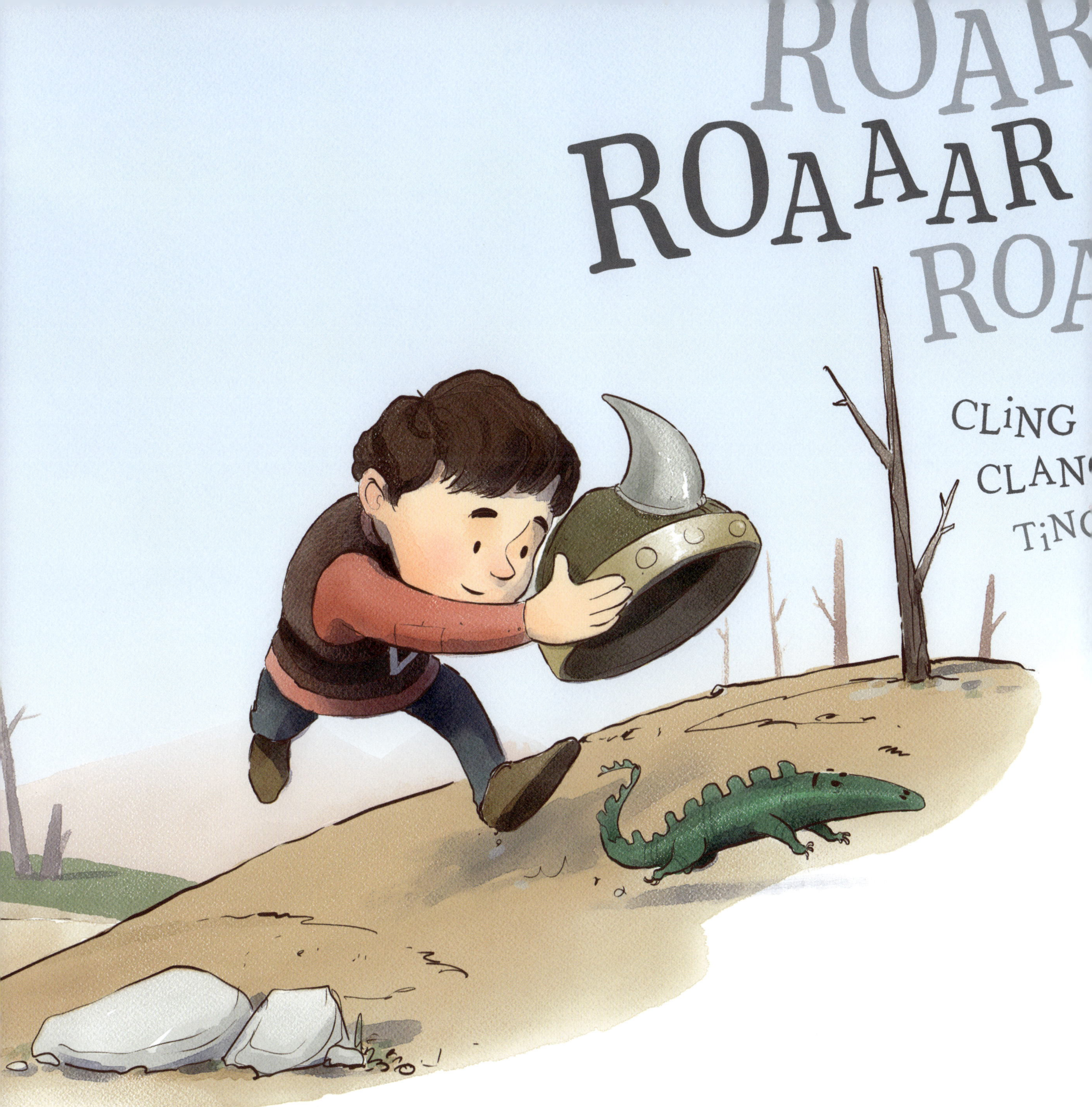

Boy ran right into the middle of it all.

The knights were stunned. 'MOVE!' they shouted.

'GET OUT OF THE WAY, BOY!' ordered the king.

'ROAR!' bellowed the dragon.

But, of course, Boy couldn't hear them.

Flames flared from the dragon's nostrils.

The knights waved their swords frantically as they marched over to Boy.

'Why aren't you listening?' shouted the king.

Boy was surprised when he looked up and saw them all. He watched them for a moment, then made his hands dance.

The knights were flabbergasted.
The king was puzzled.
The dragon was mystified.

CLiNG
CLANG
CHiNG
tiNG!
tiNG!
toNG!

Boy could see that they didn't understand him, so he took a sword and wrote in the sand.

FIGHTING?

There was silence until . . .

Suddenly the king pointed to the dragon. ‘He started it!’ he cried. ‘He burnt our forest!’

The dragon shook his head. ‘It was an accident,’ he roared. ‘I sneezed a fireball into the trees. I came to say sorry but your knights chased me away!’

The knights pointed to the king. 'He told us to,' they cried.

The king looked up at the dragon. 'Well, I thought you were coming to take my castle,' he said.

'Your castle is far too small for me,' the dragon replied.

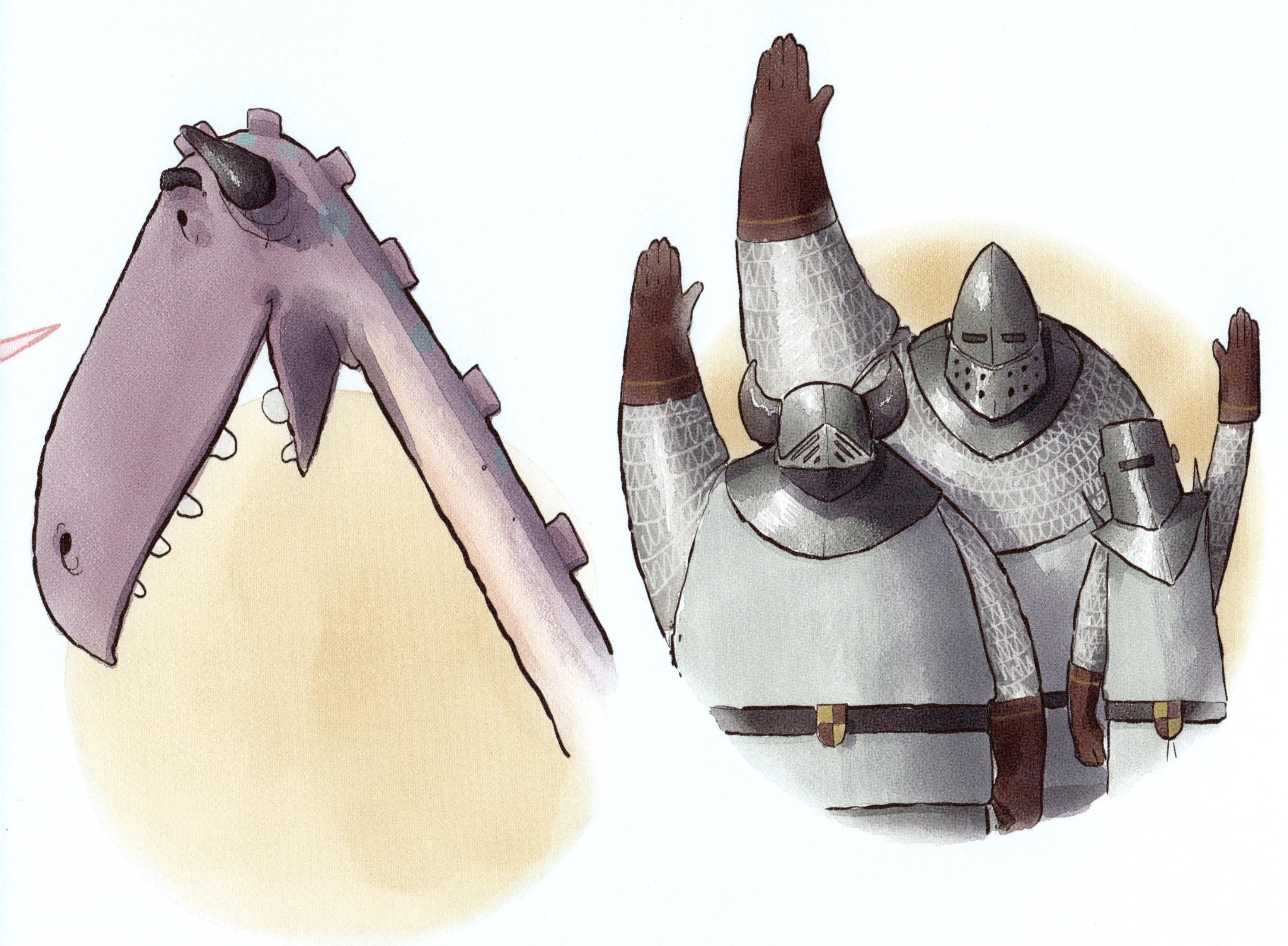

‘All I want is for you to stop chasing me. I don’t like being scared.’

‘Nor do we,’ chorused the knights.

Boy drew a picture of everyone in the sand.

He showed them how their days could be, without fighting and fear.

There was a lot of chatting and laughing.

‘I promise the knights won’t chase you anymore,’ said the king to the dragon. ‘And you can visit my castle whenever you like.’

‘And I will cover my nose when I sneeze,’ said the dragon.

Boy couldn’t hear a word, but he didn’t need to.

Back in the village,

everyone was waiting to see Boy . . .

'Thank you,' they said with dancing hands.